Snap books®

STAR BIOGRAPHIES

Selena Gomez

by Heather E. Schwartz

CAPSTONE PRESS
a capstone imprint

Snap Books are published by Capstone Press,
1710 Roe Crest Drive, North Mankato, Minnesota 56003.
www.capstonepub.com

Library of Congress Cataloging-in-Publication Data
Schwartz, Heather E.
Selena Gomez / by Heather E. Schwartz.
p. cm.—(Snap books. Star biographies)
Summary: "Describes Selena Gomez, including personal life, acting career, and music career"—Provided by publisher.
Includes bibliographical references and index.
ISBN 978-1-4296-4761-8 (library binding)
ISBN 978-1-4296-9464-3 (pbk.)
ISBN 978-1-62065-352-4 (ebook PDF)
1. Gomez, Selena, 1994– 2. Singers—United States—Biography—Juvenile literature. 3. Actors—United States—Biography—Juvenile literature. I. Title.
ML3930.G656S39 2013
791.4302'8092—dc23 [B] 2012001002

Editors: Brenda Haugen and Megan Peterson
Designer: Bobbie Nuytten
Media Researcher: Marcie Spence
Production Specialist: Kathy McColley

Photo Credits:
AdMedia: Kevan Brooks, 9; Alamy: Allstar Picture Library, cover, Litboy, 21, Pictoral Press, 6; AP images: Chris Pizzello, 17, Disney Channel/Bob D'Amico, 12, Evan Agostini, 7, Michael Underwood/PictureGroup, 16, Sipa via A Images, 26; Capstone: 28; Corbis: Nancy Kaszerman/Zuma Press, 5; Getty Images: Adam Rose/Disney Channel, 13, James Devaney/WireImage, 15, K Mazur/TCA 2008/WireImage, 27, Lisa Lake/WireImage for Kmart, 29, OutOfSightMedia/BuzzFoto.com, 10; The Kobal Collection: CS2 Films, 19; Landov: Disney Channel/MCT, 22, Rune Hellestad/UPI, 25; Newscom: 20th Century Fox, 24, PacificCoastNews, 23

Essential content terms are **bold** and are defined at the bottom of the page where they first appear.

Printed in the United States of America in North Mankato, Minnesota.
042012 006682CG12

Table of Contents

CHAPTER 1

Walking the Red Carpet

An excited crowd chanted and screamed outside AMC Loews Lincoln Square Theater in New York City on June 23, 2011. Dressed in a low-cut, light blue **chiffon** gown, Selena Gomez had just arrived for the **premiere** of her new movie, *Monte Carlo*. She accented her dress with Casadei pumps, a dainty gold bracelet, and a sparkling gold clutch. She wore her hair loose and wavy.

"I got paired with the most beautiful girls and the sweetest girls. And who can complain about shooting in Paris?"

—Selena on her costars at the premiere of *Monte Carlo,* from an interview with *TV Guide.*

chiffon—a sheer fabric made especially of silk
premiere—the first public showing of a film

Selena stepped up her style for the premiere of her movie *Monte Carlo*.

Walking the red carpet, Selena spoke with reporters. They asked about her favorite memories making the movie and her future plans. She was surrounded by celebrities, including costars Katie Cassidy and Andie McDowell.

Inside the theater, singer Justin Bieber kissed Selena's hand before taking his seat beside her. The couple snuggled and shared popcorn as they watched Selena play two leading roles on the big screen.

In the film Selena played Grace, a girl who gets mistaken for a British heiress. She also played the role of the heiress.

Selena enjoyed filming with costars Katie Cassidy (left) and Andie McDowell (right).

"Being able to do what I've always wanted to do my entire life is a gift, and my whole dream has come true. To see where I am, from where I was, is just crazy!"

—Selena in an interview with *Teen* magazine.

CHAPTER 2

A Star Is Born

Selena Marie Gomez was born on July 22, 1992. Her parents, Mandy Teefey and Ricardo Gomez, raised her in a small home in Grand Prairie, Texas. Mandy was only 16 when Selena was born. Mandy and Ricardo named their daughter after the Mexican-American singer Selena Quintanilla Perez.

Although Selena was an only child, she didn't grow up alone. "My grandmother babysat 13 kids at once. I grew up with a bunch of kids around me," she has said.

"[My mom] was really strong around me. Having me at 16 had to have been a big responsibility. My mom gave up everything for me, had three jobs, supported me, sacrificed her life for me."

—Selena in an interview with *E!*

Selena caught the acting bug from her mom, Mandy (left).

For fun, Selena's mom performed in local theater. Selena loved watching her put on makeup. She helped her mom learn her lines. Sometimes Selena even gave her mom tips after the performances.

When Selena was 5 years old, her parents divorced. Her mom's strength helped Selena to stay positive. "My [role model] is first and foremost my mom," she has said.

Sometimes Selena wanted to be a doctor or cheerleader. But other days she wanted to perform. Her favorite movie was *The Wizard of Oz*. Judy Garland, who played Dorothy, inspired Selena to become an actress.

Selena's first chance to **audition** came when producers of the show *Barney & Friends* needed a new cast. The audition was on her birthday. Shy, 7-year-old Selena was scared to see 1,400 other kids waiting to try out. But when it was her turn, she relaxed. She realized that auditioning was just like running lines with her mom. After a few callbacks, Selena won the role of Gianna on the show.

Selena visited a Hollywood, California, art gallery in 2008 with Mandy (left) and stepfather Brian Teefey (right).

Kid on Camera

Singing, dancing, and acting on *Barney* taught Selena how to take direction and perform in front of a camera. Two years later, she was ready to move on. She filmed commercials, but there wasn't much work in Texas.

When she was 11, Selena was discovered by the Disney Channel in a nationwide talent search. Producers chose her to appear in a new Disney **pilot**. The pilot wasn't picked up, but Selena did get the chance to guest star on *The Suite Life of Zack & Cody*. She also won small roles in the movies *Spy Kids 3-D: Game Over* and *Walker, Texas Ranger: Trial by Fire*.

"I realized I wanted to do comedy when I guest starred on *The Suite Life*. I was 12, and I played a small part. I heard the audience laugh, and it became addictive to me. I was like, 'Whoa, I just made them laugh.'"

—Selena in an interview with *Seventeen* magazine.

audition—to try out for a role in a TV show
pilot—a sample episode of a planned TV show

Big Break

In 2007 Selena got her big break. After auditioning several times, she landed a part on the Disney TV show *Wizards of Waverly Place*. Selena would play the role of Alex Russo, a wizard in training.

Winning the part meant Selena, her mom, and her stepfather, Brian, would have to move to California. Leaving behind her Texas home, her father, and her friends wasn't easy. But Selena was determined to follow her dreams. Her family supported her new career. They drove her to interviews and made sure she stayed grounded while surrounded by celebrities.

Selena costarred with Jake T. Austin, Jennifer Stone, and David Henrie (left to right) on *Wizards of Waverly Place.*

David DeLuise (second from left) played Jerry Russo, the father of Selena's character.

Texas Treat

When Selena left her home state, she didn't give up her love of Southern food. Living in California, she was still able to enjoy one of her favorite snacks, Texas popcorn. To make it she shakes up popcorn with salt and Tabasco sauce. Then she dips the popcorn in pickle juice before popping the kernels into her mouth.

CHAPTER 3

Life as a Celebrity

Starring on *Wizards of Waverly Place* changed Selena's life. She worked Monday through Friday. Instead of going to school she studied five hours a day on the **set**. Selena sometimes missed being in a classroom with other kids. She also missed taking science class, her favorite subject. But homeschooling helped her concentrate on her career. She announced earning her high school diploma in May 2010 on her Facebook page.

Selena found that stardom has its perks. She earned $10,000 per episode during the show's first season and enjoyed her weekly allowance of $150 to $250. She shopped mainly at Aldo and Forever 21. She also stocked up on her favorite Converse shoes. And she loved getting her hair and makeup done. She got to wear the latest fashions for magazine photo shoots.

set—the stage scene where the action is taking place, such as a kitchen or a mountaintop

Selena adds skinny jeans and bracelets to dress up her casual outfits.

"I do understand that I can't wear jeans and sneakers to an event, but I'm not a dress girl. I can't do dresses or extreme high heels. So I find my own way of dressing up!"

—Selena talking about style to *PBS Kids*.

In 2009 *Wizards of Waverly Place* won the Emmy Award for Outstanding Children's Program.

Once *Wizards* aired in October 2007, Selena couldn't go to the mall or the movies without being recognized. Fans and the **media** became interested in her love life and her famous friends, including actress Demi Lovato. She tried to steer interviews toward her career and happy events in her life. She talked about her love of old movies and her favorite foods—pizza and fried pickles. Selena even shared that she had a crush on actor Shia LeBeouf.

media—TV, radio, newspapers, and other communication forms that send out messages to large groups of people

Selena's Style

Unlike many teen celebrities, Selena prefers sneakers and jeggings to slinky dresses and high heels. When Hollywood events require more formal clothes, Selena steps it up. But even when dressed up, she makes sure she's comfortable. For the Nickelodeon Kids' Choice Awards in 2010, she wore a yellow chiffon dress with a gold beaded belt. Gold gladiator sandals, a gold oval-shaped clutch, and loosely braided hair finished off her look.

Selena also shared her desire for comfy fashion in 2010. Kmart produced Selena's "Dream Out Loud" line in July. Bright, fun prints on skirts, T-shirts, sweaters, and purses show off Selena's ability as a designer.

Selena was named one of the Best Dressed at the 2010 Nickelodeon Kids' Choice Awards.

CHAPTER 4

The Career of a Celebrity

Selena had no problem scoring more projects once *Wizards* became popular. In 2008 she voiced the character of Helga in *Horton Hears a Who*. She also guest starred in three episodes of *Hannah Montana*. She played Mikayla, Hannah's **rival** and Miley's friend.

Later that year she signed on to star in the straight-to-DVD movie *Another Cinderella Story*. Selena was nervous. It was her first leading movie role. And she had to dance! She took dancing lessons for two months. She learned the steps for the movie in a matter of weeks.

rival—someone whom a person competes against

In *Another Cinderella Story,* Selena played a high school student who wants to become a dancer.

With a whirlwind work schedule, Selena's career sometimes became her social life. In July 2008 she celebrated her 16th birthday. She ate her favorite red velvet cake with her production crew. Afterward they finished shooting a music video for the *Another Cinderella Story* **soundtrack**. Her birthday present from her mom, a black Ford Escape hybrid car, was the highlight of her big day.

Another Cinderella Story premiered in September 2008. Selena was calm at her first premiere for her own project. She arrived at the Pacific Grove Theater in Los Angeles ready to meet the press. Her steel-gray pleated dress and open-toed sandals were a hit on the red carpet.

"This is the first lead role that I took, and it's very nerve-wracking for me. I learned so much from everyone, and I hope that this is successful for all of those people."

—Selena at the premiere of *Another Cinderella Story*, from an interview with About.com.

soundtrack—a recording of music from a movie or play

Selena looked stylish at the premiere of *Another Cinderella Story*.

A Busy Princess

Next Selena traveled to Puerto Rico for a lead role in the Disney TV movie *Princess Protection Program.* This job didn't feel like work, since her best friend, Demi Lovato, was her costar. Selena thought it was strange to act in scenes pretending not to know her friend. They were busy filming and recording songs for the soundtrack. But the pair found time to have fun too. They went snorkeling in the sea and talked on the beach. They had sleepovers in Demi's hotel room. After the movie wrapped, Selena wasn't home long before she went back to Puerto Rico. This time she would be filming *Wizards of Waverly Place: The Movie.*

Selena enjoyed filming *Wizards of Waverly Place: The Movie* in Puerto Rico.

Even when she wasn't working, Selena stayed busy. She attended movie premieres, wrap parties, and awards events. She even started her own production company, July Moon Productions. Selena stayed grounded by sticking to her mom's rules: Always bring a parent to celebrity events and be back by 11:30 p.m. She also had chores to do at home. Taking out the trash and cleaning her room were only a couple of Selena's responsibilities.

Puppy Love

While in Puerto Rico, Selena was heartbroken to see the number of stray dogs. She used her celebrity status to host a fund-raising event in San Juan. At the event volunteers fed and played with the stray dogs. The event raised $17,000 for Island Dog, a rescue organization in Puerto Rico. Selena even adopted a dog. Her new pet, Chazz, had a broken leg after being hit by a car. Selena brought him home to live with her four other dogs, Willie, Wallace, Chip, and Fina.

CHAPTER 5

The Legacy

Life didn't slow down for Selena in 2009. She flew to Vancouver, Canada, in mid-April to film her first big-screen movie, *Ramona and Beezus*. For her work, she received a paycheck of $65,000. Selena loved the challenge of portraying Beezus, who was quite different from Alex Russo. And she had a fan on set—Joey King, who played her sister Ramona, loved *Wizards*! While on set, Selena posted a video blog on YouTube called "A Big Sister's Guide to Making a Movie."

Selena and her *Ramona and Beezus* costar Joey King (right) became fast friends.

Selena and her band, shown here at a 2010 London show, travel the world to play their music.

Selena also held auditions to put together a band, which she named The Scene. Selena told the media the name was a comeback to some mean-spirited comments that she was a "wannabe scene." Instead of getting upset, Selena figured she'd make a joke of it. "Anybody who tries to bring me down only inspires me," she has said.

Selena Gomez & The Scene's **debut** album was called *Kiss & Tell.* Released in September 2009, the album sold more than 66,000 copies its first week. In March 2010 the album reached gold status, with more than 500,000 copies sold. A year later, her band had produced another album.

Selena Gomez & The Scene won the award for Favorite Breakout Artist at the 2011 People's Choice Awards.

debut—a first showing

Selena chatted with celebs Demi Lovato (left) and Miley Cyrus (middle) at the 2008 Teen Choice Awards.

As a young star Selena was often compared to Demi Lovato, Taylor Swift, and Miley Cyrus. But Selena made her own mark as a multi-talented teen. With her Mexican heritage, she worked hard to gain respect as a Latina actress. She also liked representing her home state of Texas.

"I think that it's part of the job where you turn into a role model. It's not something I aimed toward. But now that it's kind of a title, I do embrace it, because it's very sweet to have little girls have posters and T-shirts of you."

—Selena on being a role model, from an interview with *Parade* magazine.

Future Plans

In July 2010 Selena celebrated her 18th birthday at a Texas-style barbecue bash with hamburgers, hot dogs, cheesy potatoes, and more than 250 friends. A few months later, she filmed the final episode of *Wizards of Waverly Place*.

Ending the show was sad, but Selena kept busy. In 2011 her latest movie, *Monte Carlo*, premiered. Her third album, *When the Sun Goes Down*, was released in June. She was working on a signature fragrance too.

Selena is considering how she'll fit future studies into her busy life. She has an interest in going to culinary school. Northwestern University is her first choice for college. She may study theater and journalism through online courses.

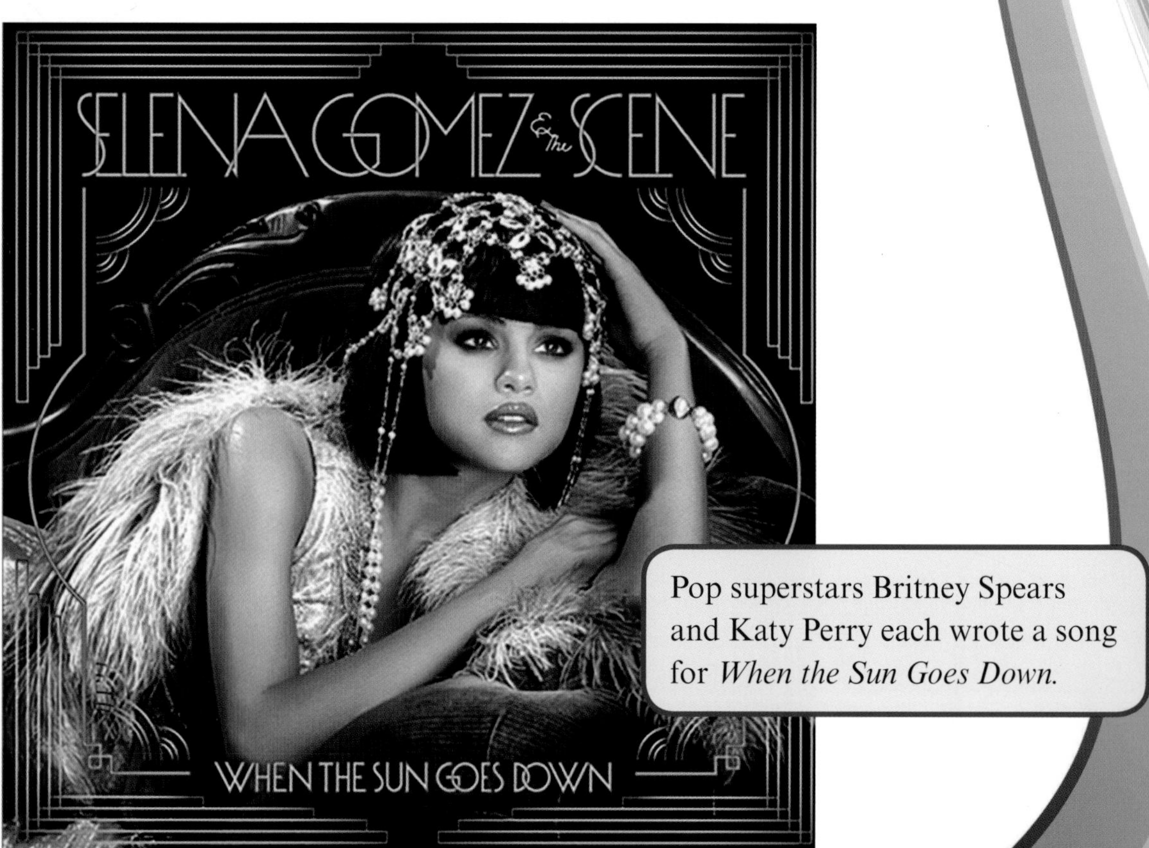

Pop superstars Britney Spears and Katy Perry each wrote a song for *When the Sun Goes Down.*

Selena, shown here signing autographs at a Philadelphia Kmart in August 2011, enjoys meeting her fans.

Selena also wants to continue in the entertainment business. She is working on a Spanish-language album. She recently completed work on the animated movie *Hotel Transylvania*. Adam Sandler and Cee Lo Green also voiced characters in the film. "I have an audience. The audience I have now, I want them to grow with me. I want to make a transition," she has said. "I want to learn and grow."

Selena already has a lifetime of success behind her. Now she's ready to work on her dreams for the future.

Glossary

audition (aw-DISH-uhn)—to try out for a role in a TV show, movie, or play

chiffon (shih-FON)—a sheer fabric made especially of silk

debut (day-BYOO)—a first showing

media (MEE-dee-uh)—TV, radio, newspapers, and other communication forms that send out messages to large groups of people

pilot (PYE-luht)—a sample episode of a planned TV show

premiere (pruh-MIHR)—the first public performance of a film, play, or work of music or dance

rival (RYE-vuhl)—someone whom a person competes against

set (SET)—the stage scene where the action is taking place, such as a kitchen or a mountaintop

soundtrack (SOUND-trak)—a recording of music from a movie or play

Read More

Azzarelli, Ally. *Selena Gomez: Latina TV and Music Star.* Hot Celebrity Biographies. Berkeley Heights, N.J.: Enslow Publishers, 2012.

Reusser, Kayleen. *Selena Gomez.* A Robbie Reader. Hockessin, Del.: Mitchell Lane Publishers, 2010.

Williams, Zella. *Selena Gomez: Actress and Singer.* Hispanic Headliners. New York: PowerKids Press, 2011.

Internet Sites

FactHound offers a safe, fun way to find Internet sites related to this book. All of the sites on FactHound have been researched by our staff.

Here's all you do:

Visit *www.facthound.com*

Type in this code: 9781429647618

Check out projects, games and lots more at **www.capstonekids.com**

Index